# Infinity

METAL(HE)ART 2023

# METAMORTHARSIS

Written by

Marcus Myers


2022-2023

# Table of contents

# 7 Weeks

When I was first admitted to the closed ward
I didn't really believe in a cure
I immediately felt evil energy
Minus laden, I'll never make it here

Crammed together with 35 crazy people
The nurses often had to hold you down
Psychotic, agonic and depressed
Manic, catatonic or aggressive

Then they started with the healing injections
Pushed down, I had to sit still
Somehow I got into a strange mood
After a week I woke up again

But Haldol is our most potent drug!
He says that so easily, the stupid white coat
The eyes, the tongue, the body are spasming
There really are no words for it

Want to sit, want to lie down, walk, sit again
Side effect of the devil's injections
I beg for the antidote
Don't get in line, the rude answer

Trapped as if behind prison walls
Dangers lurk everywhere
Deprived of my own freedom
And life as if sucked dry

Time seemed to stand still here
Just wouldn't pass

All strength is gone
Wicked wounds in my soul

I can no longer bear it all
Screaming like a spit roast
Let me go, I want to get out of here
I just can't stand it here any longer

I'm being put to bed
Tied up, black night
A few hours pass
They pay no attention to me on their rounds

But when visitors came, they were in need
I was quickly given the antidote
No one should see me like this
Visitors should leave satisfied

I was in there for 7 weeks
It changed my whole inside
And today I really realize
That I was in hell

Epilogue

And if there's anyone else out there
Still angry at me, pissed off
Let me tell you: I was tormented
And had to pay for every single sin

A Raven

I see a raven on the curb
It seems to have something in its beak
I suspect something and stop
There's something great to see in a moment

He's taken his time
Looks around to see if any cars are coming
Suddenly a nut flies in a high arc
And hits the gray road surface

The first car comes along too
Drive over the nut, I really wish it would
Bad luck, unfortunately it missed it,
The second time it crashed

Now the raven flies to his nut
I give him a kiss goodbye
The bird made my day
I'm no longer chained to bad thoughts

The best things in life are free
You just have to make an effort
If you see them with love and heart
Then sometimes the pain goes away

A Walk

I take a walk through the streets again
Letting my mind wander a little
It's evening and very quiet
Enjoying the peace and quiet is what I want

I see the lights, the trees, the bushes
The flowers, the stars, the moon and the houses
What might be going on behind the walls?
Love, hate, violence against women?

Violence against children and men?
I have to calm down, I wish I could change it
Once upon a time there must have been great love
But for many, it's only great torment

There is spitting, beating, biting
Brute force, without conscience
How is it with togetherness
Why is it so often doomed to destruction

Over time, you lose all fear and respect
Now feelings of hatred have come to life
Why do you do this to yourselves
You're better off on separate paths

Such big dreams with a future and a plan
Now you're all just sick of each other
Where is the love, the tenderness, the heart?
All that's left is endless pain

Let go and give more freedom
Too many constraints in too many lifes

Is it selfish? No, rather healthy
Everyone needs space, then things run more smoothly

Now I'm slowly going back home
There's no violence there, what luck
I see my brother, smile at him
He just wants his rest too

Which way?

Who shows me the way
How life goes?
Never learned anything like that
Was far removed from education
The other young ones rebel
I'm about to lose myself
What should I do, what should I not do
What decisions should I make?

How should I do what I never learned
The one so far away from the world
I have often received gifts
But advice only rarely heard

Who is to blame for my misery?
Mother and father, whom I do not honor?
Life is a real torture
Society, fate, genetic material?

It's always the others, alas!
Is it really that simple?
Isn't it myself?
Who likes to pass the blame on to others?

Yes, you don't like responsibility
Now it's up to you to decide for yourself
Now you are great, your own master
It's your life, here you go!
Make decisions with courage
Some things go wrong, others go well!

The irony in this story
There is no concrete guideline
We ourselves only have to choose
Which values count for us
A virtue from which we have distanced ourselves
The living out of our own values

## Psychosis (Station 8)

The night is pitch black, inside me and outside
Something compels me, I have to go outside.
It's Satan screaming at me
It has to be today, I'm ready.

The road is long, demons at the edge
With black eyes, he will not spare me
He wants to feast on my sins
I'm already dead, dead and buried.

What was I looking for, what drove me?
What has God written in his book?
So many demons that live in my soul
Can no one ever forgive me?

I have done so much wrong
Closed ward, station 8

On my way to being crucified
About to die of fear
A look into the sky, there is a light
Near and far, I don't understand it

Is it trying to tell me to go back?
The devil is tearing you apart, piece by piece
It's too late, the soul has died
Now I've become a demon myself

What was I looking for, what drove me?
What has God written in his book?
So many demons that live in the soul
Can no one ever forgive me?

I have done so much wrong
Closed ward, station 8

Born to die! Born to live?
Born to die! Born to live?

What was I looking for, what drove me?
What did God write in his book?
So many demons living in my soul
Can no one ever forgive me?

I have done so much wrong
Veins open, status: night!

Fear and Panic

I'm standing in the marketplace, surrounded by people
Now the fear takes hold, can't fight it
The sweat forms trickling beads
Now I just want to get away from here

Now I am seized by the wildest panic
I lose control, methods don't work at all
I just want to run away quickly
No, I can't face my fear today

Fear is your friend, it wants to protect you
It's been useful for thousands of years
Only sometimes it overdoes it far too much
No less and no more!

Should you learn alternative reactions?
Yes, but not in irrational cases
Sometimes you can train your brain
Sometimes the only thing that helps is learning to
accept!

Now I stand in the darkest darkness
Is there not a slight sparkle?
Offer Satan your throat
Come now, take my soul!

Take it now, or leave me forever!
Yes, I think I'm free of my fear now
I've already won once
Yes, but only once, it will come again

Fear is your friend, it wants to protect you

It's been useful for thousands of years
Only sometimes it overdoes it far too much
No less and no more!

Should you learn alternative reactions?
Yes, but not in irrational cases
Sometimes you can train your brain
Sometimes the only thing that helps is learning to accept!

But it could be...
But it could be......
But it could..........!

This thought will never give you freedom
And will always be a hindrance!
Dare with courage, try as much as you can
What have you got to lose but fear?

Suicide and Depression

Months already the rope around my neck
Always searching for the place of my fall
Can't take it anymore, my life and myself
Don't want to live anymore, I can't stand it

Everything is dark, blacker than black
No one can help me, not even a doctor
Lost faith in me and everyone
Otherwise there will be no salvation

Do I take pills, the blade, the rope?
The devil has fucked me in the ass
I'm the scum of the earth
Hope I'll never rise again!

Everyone hates me, especially myself
Who is constantly rolling in pain
Lost friends, I can understand
Shouldn't they all go down with me

Was called a sissy back then
The one who said it recognized it well
What I still needed was the last kick
She broke my neck with it

Do I take pills, the blade, the rope?
The devil fucked me in the ass
I'm the scum of the earth
Hope I'll never rise again!

Now you want to do the same?
Try not to wake up?

You shouldn't go this early without a fight
The soul can die, but it can also rise again!
I've been through the whole thing myself
You see, it didn't bring me death

Death is not the solution to the problem
Because energy will always continue to exist
Get through, if possible difficult time
Depression is such a nasty disease!

Not your fault, you're out of it
Nobody chooses this !!!!

Too young and too naive

When I was still young I met a girl
A full appliance, you could call it
Then it really happened like that
She took an interest in me

Over time, we learned to love each other
It didn't just remain a friendship
Our love really went very, very far
We spent an endless amount of time together

When we were together, I was whole
It was an inner dance of joy
After a year and a few days
I was overcome by a feeling of unease

Was it really me she loved
Or only the one when I bent myself
Different clothes, different behavior
Only with deception could I keep her

I no longer dared to say anything
I didn't want to risk losing her
When I was as I should be
I realized that she didn't want me anymore

I was partly to blame, I didn't stay true to myself
Love fell by the wayside
I let myself be blinded by her beauty
That can quickly turn into the opposite

I want to be loved for who I really am
Then the whole thing makes sense

Just need to be myself, inside and out
Then maybe a few out there will like me

# What remains

Wounds heal, souls live
Will never give you more love
When a part of me weeps silently
There is no common ground

Can see again, eyes open
Secrets are now revealed
No more blackness, no more demons
No more blindness, no more deception

Mirror, mirror on the wall
A seal branded on the forehead
Mirror, mirror on the wall
Got lost in demons

Is that me in this mirror,
My, your projection ?
Completely scarred after our journey
Never again in your dark way

Nor from you and not from others
Walk on clouds of true love
Can now see, the seal healed
Space only for me in this mirror

Times show new ways,
Out of the darkness into the light
To persevere standing too little,
old scars do not break me

Mirror, mirror on the wall
A seal branded on my forehead
Mirror, mirror on the wall

Got lost in demons

What remains ?

- Forgiveness

Reality

There is a question that often arises
Is there matter or just an imaginary world?
Is there anything out there at all
Or is the brain just having fun ?

My brain is in a closed room
Is it the matrix, I don't think so
In all this time, it has heard a lot
But has everything arrived correctly?

Actually, I perceive almost only vibrations
Should I believe everything I once saw?
Or is it just distorted
Could it be that my brain is wrong ?

Is there only my own reality
Or is there something that stands against it ?
There are 8 billion worlds
Which oppose me.

Am I the only one who knows the truth
And does not recognize other truths ?
Narcissistically blinded, do not accept others
We all live in different worlds

The Nightmare (Sleep paralysis)

I lie in bed and wake up
And open my eyes
It feels like something is sitting on me
And I wonder what it is

I have trouble moving
Something seems to be wrapped around my neck
It presses my neck heavily into the pillow
What's going on, I need to know

I try to reach for the lamp
Then the great fear will probably give way
I press the button, the light doesn't come on
I try again and again, despairing

Suddenly I'm standing in front of my brother's door
But he's not here at all
Then I'm standing in the dark stairwell
How did I actually get out of here

Then I seem to be lying in bed again
And arm flying to the lamp
Press the button, the light goes on
Think to myself, it was almost your turn

Now I'm sitting on the edge of the bed
That was nothing nice at all
I think about it, I'm not sure
I wonder if that was the nightmare?

(The painter Johann Heinrich Füssli painted several
versions of the Nightmare)

Friendship and Love

Nobody understands you, you feel alone
Nobody wants to be with you
You're like a freak, an outsider
Don't know what to do on your own

You open your mouth, big laugh
I understand such things
Want to be loved for who you are
The others don't recognize your soul

And if you're wrong, I don't care
I'm still always loyal to you
That's what I meant back then
When I told you I was on your side

You have so much to give
I can experience the greatest things with you
Nobody sees you in the streets
They seem abandoned by empathy

They feel better, make others small
That seems necessary to be elevated
I look into you, your big heart
But unfortunately also so much pain

And if you're wrong, I don't care
I'm still always loyal to you
That's what I meant back then
When I told you I was on your side

I've learned to feel loved
From a woman with real feelings

Accepted me from the start
When real love slowly began

It's been over 25 beautiful years
Far more than other couples
If you're in a bad way, I'm not far away
I thank you from the bottom of my heart for the
wonderful time!

Exorcism

I wanted to be human, completely normal
Was brought up Catholic, with morals
With goals, values, love and moderation
Religious, if against it, met with hate!

I did everything they taught me
It was Jesus we worshipped
Suppressed desires, just as you wanted
Was always as I should be!

You want my name? Shall I call it?
I'm terrified, can't you recognize it?
I have so many, why do you ask me?
Does your church Latin let you down like this?

Oh Lord my Savior, please save me!
Again and again verses, again and again
Hitler, Judas, Cain and Ba'al!
Roman rituals? Fuck you!

By your robes, I soaked myself
Why did you have to be so soulless?
All I ever perceived, still close
Survives in my brain, still there

You hold me tight, in my bed
Surrounded by prayers, naked fear that tugs at me
You keep talking to me
My reaction, what should it be?

You want my name? Should I say it?
I'm panicking, can't you recognize it?

I have so many, why are you asking me?
Is your church Latin letting you down like this?

Oh Lord my Savior, please save me!
Again and again verses, again and again
Hitler, Judas, Cain and Ba'al!
Roman rituals? Fuck you!

I'll tell you my only name now:
Anneliese! Well, priest, can you take it?
Just a human being, abandoned by everyone
If only you had let me be human

Epilogue

Finally, I must mention Arnold Renz and accomplices
Always keep a candle burning....!
Grave desecrated! Until then you have done it
But where is your prophesied miracle?

(For Anneliese Michel * September 21, 1952 † July 1,
1976)

Demon Demon

How is a demon created
From things we do really bad
How others act wickedly with us
So we too walk in great sin

Do they really come from hell?  No!
They must have originated in the inner abyss!
Deep in the soul they find life
The hatred we give each other

Covetousness, greed, all seven sins
Everyone acts for selfish reasons
Does this have anything to do with God
No, only we humans inflict evil on each other

Where is this God when you need him
After all, you breathed life into us
You dare us to do too much
Oh Jesus, give me my peace

So you are love, are you?
Then why is there so much pain?
Here on your beloved earth
That I may be born again

Without pain, without torment
That must be a human idea
What helps the soul in distress
Forgiveness is the antidote

Separation, violence, hatred and all evil
Wants me to redeem myself

Forgiving yourself is so hard
I choose love, thank you very much!

Is the resurrection really true
When I saw the soul die ?
One thing I will not give up,
Dear people I have met !

# Question of all Questions

Zero and one, binary system
This truth seems to exist
Is there a mirror image of everyone?
In an inverted world?

In a parallel universe it could be
Me upside down from head to toe
Everything that is good in my life
Could exist there as evil

Since the beginning of time
This question has divided us
Everyone wants to know the truth
Without ever naming proofs

Philosophy and religions try to explain
Or only to transfigure all people ?
All answers are vague
There is no answer to the ultimate question

Is there the Matrix, God's plan ?
Have people just lost their way ?
Hawking once described it like this :
If you dig a hole, you get a hill !

As long as we live, let's believe Kant
He recognized possible matter
When we are dead, when we bite the dust
Will we perhaps know something more !?

Shadows need light

Constantly these shadows, they live in me
God, is this a punishment from you
Or is it just me punishing myself
Actually without any need

If so many demons live in me
The devil will not spare me
But every shadow needs its light
Why didn't I realize that before

The demon with the many names
I gave him my amen too often
A rebellion germinates in me
The light helps me to defend myself

What is the light, what is the shadow
Things we had not forgiven ourselves for
There is so much light in me
Yes, Satan now you're getting pissed off

Enough with the fear
Running against blindness
What I couldn't see before
Is the good that was in me before

Everything has a counterpart
With fear it is happiness
Just as darkness needs light
A god also needs something like you

I'll get rid of you, you can believe me
I will no longer allow you so much power

There is something that creates trust
A love that makes fear unnecessary

A trust, little mustard seed big
You are so truly soulless
I will be loved as I am
That really makes sense then

Now I'm on my own
Does a relationship really have to be
Be yourself, stay at the bottom
Then love will eventually win

In the beginning, sworn, unending love
In the end only endless blows
I won't get involved in that anymore
It must be loyal, genuine love

However great love may be
It often ends in a day
It's sad, a downfall
But also always a new beginning

So now I have written this
What have I learned, what has remained
Love, light, human fall
Fear is ok, I am myself

What do demons want?

I've long wondered why my demons won't leave me
alone.

What do they want from me and why don't they just go
away?
Or am I just holding on to them myself?
I have done a lot wrong in my life,
But why keep feeding the demons?

Did I really have no life at all?
Or just always striving for the big picture ?
This „Faust" in us is no helper
And never a giver of peace!

Theodor Fontane showed me,
It was not just wasted time
I had a really right life
I just have to forgive everyone and myself.

Now I know what my demons want from me !

My love, my light and my forgiveness.

They are welcome to have that. : )

# Agony of the Devil

Why was he kicked out of heaven in the first place
Did he only think he knew something else
Is not allowed his own opinion
With her adored Serene Highness

The church preaches forgiveness and love
Jesus received unbearable blows from people
Church wants to impose faith on everyone
Blame for the end of cultures and eras

The church has never apologized
I really wonder which god it worships
A good one or an evil one
How will the church resolve this

Some sins are allowed to those who are called
They like to look the other way
There is a transfer, there is forgiveness
Pastors are devils in so many lives

So now we are at the point
How it really works with the devil
The devil is elevated to seducer
So the priest-man is forgiven

Washed clean from sins
Washed clean for selfish reasons
Is this now a plan from the devil
Or are church leaders just bad people

Is this offense a terrible sin
That would suit the devil

Or is it still the fear
Without church indulgences

Money, power, sex and politics
A pope really needs a lot of skill
Why did Pope Benedict
So suddenly buckled

Did he know more than others
Devil in Vatican land
But is protected by the military
Jesus' help was of no use

The devil lives in his agony
God has never forgiven him
Many people live inwardly broken
Did the devil or a human being break them?

The devil lives in unbearable grief
And I am often really angry with God
The tempter, he has often tempted me
And my doubting seems so wicked

The devil has shown me much
Would be ready for a better life
But I have not failed
Said no to this one

Yes, the devil is a part of us
Has no favor of trust with me
Let us live in peace
But the church has wasted its giving

The learned church measure
Tells me that I don't fit in

The evil devil's favorite prey
Are hypocritical church people

Epilogue

The hardest thing in life,
To learn to forgive yourself
There is no devil, there are only people
Guilt, trauma, abuse and hypocrisy

My trust in Jesus goes as far
As far as I can, in my humanity
The soul is a delicate thing
That's why Jesus is so gentle with us

Mirror

You stand lost in front of a mirror
A seal seems to be branded on your forehead
666 it seems to call
To recognize only evil in it

What have I done, I am so lost
Evil thoughts in my ears
Have left the real world
Black hands that grasp me

But everything is so familiar
I feel comfortable in my own skin
Relatives want to torment me
Everything is ok in my life

They seem so closely conspiring
Like I've lost control
They lie, want to give peace
Say I no longer have their blessing

They say I need help
They seem like wolves to me
In my own world
Everything is fine after all

I've seen myself reflected
My black image softened
Slowly I realize then
Your opinion could be right

The black that lives in me
Becomes so concrete in the mirror

I must have drifted off psychologically
The secret is probably out now

Must unite good and evil
Not impossible for me to solve
My brain is just an organ
Calls for help which I did not accept

Be so hard on myself'
Of a mentally ill story
But two becomes one
The essence of every human being!

Death ! A beginning ?

I was thrown into this world
Without my own will and knowledge
Whether I really wanted it myself
It was decided that I should be

Did i want to be alive
A life full of fear and pain
No one ever asked me that
I was told it was a gift

I thought I'd get a great life
Full of happiness, after great striving
After 20 years on earth
I knew I'd be nothing

Mental death, fear, paranoia
Sick brain that controls me
Hardly any energy to survive
Striving for the big time in my head

What I desire, I cannot have
That made me race so much
I know what it could be like
Seeing other people's lives

But then something came into play
What I really liked after all
Is what I saw, the real world
Or perfectly imagined in me

Do I really want all this
So that demons can feast on me

Is there something that forgives my failure
Perhaps a human deity

I can't trust what I see
To build on distorted input
Is everything as I see it
With blinded soul marriage

God has never broken his word
Has never promised great things
Will help me in life and soul
So that I don't torture myself so much

Do I have a life? Yes !
One that I did not see before
Was thrown into the world
Don't want to miss it anymore

We all have skeletons in the closet
No need for a plate of Fortune
What if acceptance moves in
In wounded emotional territory

Loss hurts from the marrow to the bone
But could be a new beginning
Nothing is lost in the universe
We are reborn in a different way

And the moral of this story
We don't know the answer
But something that seems possible to me
Death could be the beginning of something so great

Going shopping

I'm in a really good mood today
The only thing left to do is shopping
But something makes me wonder
I haven't showered, am i funny now

I know what's coming
My brain has never been wrong
Have courage and go anyway
The push feeling is far too great

Ok, arrived at the store
Perceived by the brain Observation
All eyes are on me
Say to myself: It's not like that

I'd better stand still
Can no longer walk straight ahead
I wonder if everyone is looking at me
I can feel it in my back

I'm the one looking after myself
That's the biggest joke of all
And if someone laughs at me
It's also appropriate at that moment

Does that say something about me or the viewer
Yes, all right, he's laughing
He doesn't even know me, it doesn't matter
We all laugh at others sometimes

That's where humor comes in
People laugh at others a lot
My vanity is far too great

Pull yourself together, let go

Is perfection oh so important
All striving for it so right
You just have to learn to be human
Not always reach for the stars

To strive for your humanity
That would really make sense
Behave like you do at home
Your honest blueprint

People aren't that bad
It's only you that breaks you
No one judges you that harshly
Only the sick soul. Yours!

Human = Pain

Sometimes I feel so alone
I want to be with someone
This person could redeem me
And give my soul peace

Is there someone who discovers me
And awakens my soul fire
Gives me the love I need
This person gets it from me too

Would that really be my salvation
Or false synapse chaining
Am I then really, really whole
With an inner soul dance of joy

No, unfortunately it's not that simple
Every connection sometimes breaks
This person can also give you pain
Stop giving in to dreams

I was someone else from the start
Wandering through life alone
Nice and bad people in my life
So much pain to forgive

But have I forgiven them
Is common use in life
Do I really want to be one of them
To destroy myself and others

Every person is alone for life
There can be so many around you

The key is to recognize
Not to run blindly after love

Only you must slowly learn
To acknowledge the truth
Not to abuse others
To give you the right to exist

Learn to cope on your own
Not to bask in admiration
Give yourself the right to live
Then the next love will be real

People often mean pain
Stop pining for great love
Being alone is not so bad
From now on become real in life

Then peace, light, joy and rest will come
No, you really haven't missed anything
Be satisfied with life itself
And with what you get from it

Recipe

So now I'll prescribe you something
Something that always suits you
It's very mild and easy to learn
To remove your self-flagellation

Yes, you used to do a lot of things wrong
But punished yourself long enough for it
Do you really want to give away
Give your life away to others

Make your life as it suits you
Let go of the eternal ballast
This ballast only survives within yourself
That is exactly what torments you so much

The others have long since forgotten
You no longer have to compete with them
They now live a life of their own
You only need to forgive yourself and them

There is one truth that always applies
What exists needs its counterpart
It cannot exist alone
It would lose its power

Do you know what is really true
If there are so many demons inside you
Then there are just as many angels inside you
Unite everything, that makes sense

You are good and you are evil
So that you can redeem yourself

Not only demons are after you
But also the entire army of angels


For mild cases: 3 times "Never mind" per day
For severe cases: 3 times "Don't give a shit" per day
For very severe cases: "So, now you can all kiss my ass" 8 times a day
It's best to find out for yourself how it helps you the most

Have you been ?

Are you a person of science
Or has religion brought knowledge
How is a demon created
From things that life does to us

Have you been beaten?
Have you been abused?
Have you been betrayed?
Have you been betrayed?
Have you been raped?
Have you been kidnapped ?
Were you left alone ?
Were you put in an incubator ?
Were you bullied ?
Were you abandoned ?
Were you exploited ?
Were you forced to do something ?
Were you ridiculed ?
Have you been abandoned?
Have you been seduced into drugs?
Have you been jealous?
Have you been separated from lovers?
Have you been rejected?
Have you been discriminated against?

Religions have a name for every demon
Not much needs to be said about that
Religion does not believe science
This belief has brought so much suffering

Every religion on this earth
Wants it to be chosen

Insists so much on its own right
Other faiths would be bad

Often fought for
Inhuman, totally disinhibited
Religion seems to be in great trouble
Killing in the name of religion

The colonels are so rich
Somehow like the mafia
Always together with the powerful
To gain the great wealth

Forbidden my own faith
The one I allow myself
Must be of the devil
The dignitary does not see that

Now I am a lost soul
That I may surrender to the devil
Abandoned, non-existent
Soul dead, excommunicated

Yes, that's how it must be
Religion needs a halo
Our lack of faith
Allow the demons to enter

But can't it be
As a human being you are a poor pig
Whatever you do is always wrong
Salvation resounds from the church

I won't settle for that
It's my life that I have

Life wants me to forgive myself
And not live in agony

# Farewell

Now you are gone, another life
So many questions have arisen
Tied to the bottom of my soul
So that I really torture myself

The thoughts circle around so much
I can no longer find the right answer
Black or white, good or evil
A riddle that I will never solve

What thoughts did you leave with
Have I become entangled in self-pity
Seeking redemption for all pain
At the end is a broken heart

Will you tell me everything later
Will i be roasted in hell
So many chances I've wasted
When affection for you began

So many things we could have done
My doing, just giving me time
How can I forgive myself
There was so much to experience with you

I didn't do it, wasted time
Suicide a possibility
But there's something that stops me
Maybe you're in the right place

There's still a chance to meet you
So we can discuss everything again

Shall we believe what Jesus said
Who never complained about his suffering

I am preparing everything for you
After death a heavenly gate
We are all united in eternal light
This does not exist for the devil

This possibility exists
Love that never perishes
A love that always forgives !
A hope that always conquers !

Perfectly imperfect

Do you want to do everything right
So that not everyone laughs at you
You really want to please them
Who mostly just talk nonsense

Am i too short, am i too fat
If I were perfect, that would be my luck
An operation would probably help
No longer the food of these wolves

Loved by really everyone and everything
That's probably worth striving for
Fuck my ego, fuck me
I am so truly disgusting

I'll take a look at it, like Schopenhauer
In abstracto, back shiver
Doing this to yourself, better any knowledge
You've thrown your life away

For your own projection
Who pays any attention to you
That's only one, that's you
Does not allow imperfections

Only one who looks at you so hard
And always observes you so critically
That is only ever simply yourself
The view that you choose

What if you ever live in concreto
And stand by yourself imperfectly

What if it's about you
What about your needs

There is a place where you have home rights
You haven't missed the jump yet
Common sense is not a good mirror
Presses the devil's seal on you

Try loving yourself
That's why I wrote this
A good piece of advice from me to you
You are only responsible for yourself

Be as you are, real gain
Just like now, that makes sense
It is never your own failure
God and life want you like this

# Torment without end - End of torment

Everything that happened to me
Has always been there in the universe
Time, matter, energy and space
The church hardly believes that

Ah, the singularity
Which exists for physicists
Denies the holy spirit
A light that shows us the way

When I look at the palms of my hands
Split path, hurts me so much
What if I turn the tables
And see the light in life

Me united in body and soul
Jesus, who forgives me
A faith not so bad
Faith that grows in me

Unite in me good and evil
All men have ways
Why not stand by me
And idly watch my downfall

I am now, united soul
No longer give honor to torment
Have found a way
I've toiled so long for it

It was not easy, I must say
My devil was after me

He brought me much torment
No choice with this illness

It all had to happen like this
Otherwise I would lose loved ones
My status quo, my life now
People have hurt me so much

I forgive everyone and myself too
Tell everyone that Jesus lives in you
Don't give up on life
Accept agony for love

Yin and yang is not stupid at all
So many blind people make me so tired
If so much evil did not live in me
Then my love would not be alive

So, the journey comes to an end
Jesus, to whom I turn
There's only one thing left for me now
Now protect the right of place, mine !!!

End

My Ego wants

- to be great
- thinks I always have to exert influence
- to be a hero
- to be like others
- not to be afraid
- be perfect
- not to be offended
- be a great engraver
- be vain
- want to consume people and things
- be strong
- to be loved
- to belong
- to be equal
- justify oneself
- wants the sensation
- can be influenced
- believes every bullshit
- is a doubter
- is desperate
- prevents me from devoting myself to Jesus
etc. etc.


But my true self is completely different.

My ego and my true self do not match.

That is a problem. Does anyone here know something like this? Does anyone have any ideas?

I no longer want to be dominated by my ego.

My ego only ever appears when I meet people !!!

It's so exhausting!

This is me

My ego and my true self are not friends.

This is me.

I want my peace, my freedom and my quiet. And I am lazy.

That is me.

I am learning to meditate now.

Kind regards,

Marcus

The final prayer

Lord,

please teach me
between my ego (I)
and my true self
to distinguish

Thank you for your grace

You are the way
You are Alpha and Omega

Right now

Please keep me in your hand

I love you !

I thank you with humility!

: )

Anything is possible

Marcus Myers Metamortharsis 2023